I.M. 1001.
Cancelling
I.C. 692.

AIR MINISTRY,
KINGSWAY,
W.C.

February, 1920

The following information is issued for the guidance of all concerned.

W. A. Robinson

By Command of the Air Council.

REPORT

ON THE

PFALZ BIPLANE (TYPE D.XV.).

The Naval & Military Press Ltd

Published by
The Naval & Military Press Ltd
5 Riverside, Brambleside, Bellbrook
Industrial Estate, Uckfield, East Sussex,
TN22 1QQ England

Tel: +44 (0) 1825 749494

Fax: +44 (0) 1825 765701

www.naval-military-press.com

www.military-genealogy.com

In reprinting in facsimile from the original, any imperfections are inevitably reproduced and the quality may fall short of modern type and cartographic standards.

I.M. 1001.
Cancelling
I.C. 692.

AIR MINISTRY,
KINGSWAY,
W.C.

February,. 1920

The following information is issued for the guidance of all concerned.

By Command of the Air Council.

REPORT

ON THE

PFALZ BIPLANE (TYPE D.XV.).

REPORT ON THE PFALZ SINGLE SEATER FIGHTER TYPE D.XV.

Two examples of this aeroplane were seen at Villacoublay, in May, 1919, both in flying condition. It appears that only a small number of this type ever reached France or Belgium. The date, 23/10/18, is marked in the centre of the lower plane.

GENERAL.

Two earlier types of Pfalz single-seaters, the D.III. and D.XII., have already been reported upon. This new model is an advance on these machines, and retains certain features of both, but incorporates so many new features that it may be regarded as a new design. It will be recalled that much of the design of the D.XII. Pfalz was evidently inspired by Fokker practice, notably the radiator and N-type interplane struts.

Until the advent of the D.XV. model, however, the Pfalz machines had retained the usual system of wire bracing for the wings, but the Fokker scheme of deep wing spars and the elimination of wire bracing is adopted in the latest Pfalz.

LEADING PARTICULARS AND DIMENSIONS.

No figures dealing with the weight of the machine are available. Contrary to the usual practice, no inscriptions dealing with weight were painted on the fuselage.

Engine	200-H.P. Bayern.
Crew	One.
Dimensions (See scale drawing at end of report):—	
Overall span	28 ft. 1½ in.
Overall length	21 ft. 0 in.
Overall height	9 ft. 3½ in.
Area of complete upper plane, with aileron	121·0 sq. ft.
Area of complete lower plane	86·0 ,,
Area of aileron	6·6 ,,
Area of aileron balance	·9 ,,
Horizontal area of fuselage	31·4 ,,
Vertical area of fuselage	58·6 ,,
Area of fin	1·0 ,,
Area of rudder	5·8 ,,
Area of rudder balance	·4 ,,
Area of fixed tail planes	16·0 ,,
Area of elevator	14·2 ,,
Area of elevator balance (both sides)	1·2 ,,
Maximum cross sectional area of body	7·0 ,,

WINGS.

General Design.—The upper plane of the Pfalz is made in one piece, as was the case with the D.III. and D.XII. models. The lower plane is also in one piece, and does not come into actual contact with the fuselage. Both upper and lower planes are attached to the fuselage by means of an arrangement of stream-line steel struts, and the two planes are inter-connected near their ends by means of N-type struts. This system of struts constitutes the sole connecting link between upper plane and lower plane, and between both planes and body ; wire bracing is entirely absent.

The natural complement to this absence of flexible bracing—a thick wing section with deep spars, is present in the Pfalz, though not to such a high degree as is the case with the Fokker D.VII.

The upper plane has its top surface horizontal, so far as the portion of wing between the interplane struts is concerned. From the interplane struts to the wing tips the upper surface rises very slightly. The taper is produced by the dihedral angle on the lower surface of the wing, and the natural result is that both trailing edge and leading edge possess a slight dihedral. Balanced ailerons are fitted to the upper plane only.

The lower plane is of smaller dimensions than the upper, and is so placed relatively to the upper plane that there is a considerable degree of stagger. Its design is precisely similar to that of the upper plane, except that the rising at the wing tips is very slight indeed.

The angle of incidence is estimated at 2 deg. for the upper plane, and 3 deg. for the lower, at the centre.

The photographs clearly show that an aluminium strip, about 7 in. wide, covers the fabric of the lower plane immediately under the fuselage, where oil and petrol are particularly liable to drip.

The various illustrations clearly show that the gap is considerably larger than usual. Up to a certain point increasing the gap serves, of course, to lessen the interference with the lift of the lower plane. Prior to 1914 the lower planes of a tractor biplane were almost invariably fitted to the bottom of the fuselage. The necessary gap was obtained by lifting the upper plane well above the pilot's head. In this position the plane necessarily interfered with the pilot's view to a considerable extent, but this was not particularly important for peace machines.

This is very different, however, in the case of fighting aeroplanes. In this machine the view is an all-important consideration, and, in order to decrease obstruction as far as possible, the upper plane was gradually lowered until it reached a position on the same level as the pilot's eyes. With the upper plane in this position it is, of course, possible for the pilot to see above and below the plane. In this connection it is interesting to note the evolution of the monoplane type into the parasol monoplane for an exactly similar reason.

So long as the lower plane is fixed to the bottom of the fuselage the lowering of the upper plane naturally decreases the gap. The Pfalz D.XV. is an attempt to get the best possible view, at the same time keeping a large gap ; and while the solution of the problem is far from new, the exact method of fixing in position planes and fuselage is interesting.

STRUTS.

It has already been mentioned that besides the Fokker type interplane struts there is a system of tubular steel struts holding the upper and lower planes respectively to the body. The upper plane is fixed to the body by an "M" strut on each side. This welded-up group of struts is very similar to that employed on the D.XII. model. There are slight differences, which may easily be recognised on reference to the photographs. The lower plane is attached to the body by two groups of three struts each (one on each side), which may be described as miniature interplane struts, since they are of the same "N" shape. Figure 1 gives a clear idea of the strutting system, and shows how the lower front attach-

FIG. 1.

ment of the lower plane and body struts is attached to the point where the rear limb of the under-carriage "V" is fixed to the fuselage. It will be readily understood that the means whereby the fuselage is fixed relatively to the planes gives adequate rigidity and is of good design. Reference to Figure 2

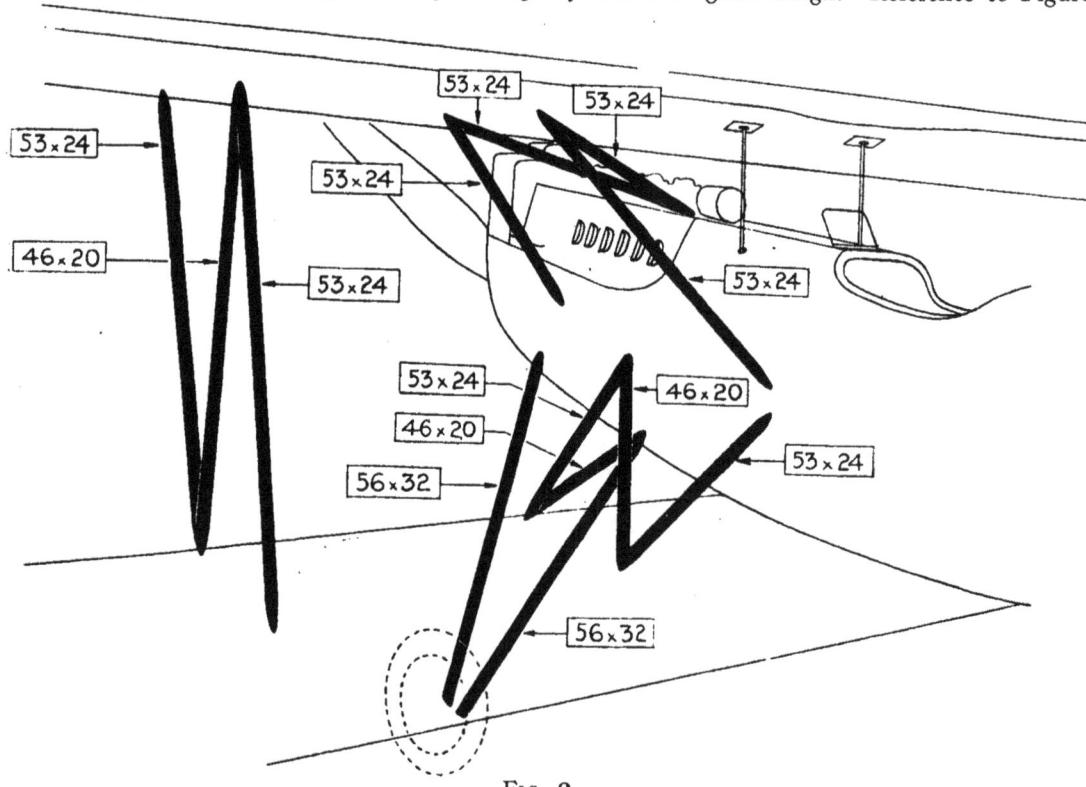

FIG. 2.

will show that the major and minor axes of the stream-line section of the hollow tubular struts are marked in figures, which represent millimetres.

The attachment of interplane struts to spars is very similar to the corresponding fitting of the Fokker D.VII., *i.e.*, a ball-headed bolt is screwed into the extremity of the strut and held in place by a lock nut. The ball drops into a socket, which forms the head of a bolt passing through the wing spar. Ball and socket are both drilled, and a pin passed through and locked by a split pin (*see* Fig. 3). This method obviously allows of adjustment, within small limits, of the length of the strut.

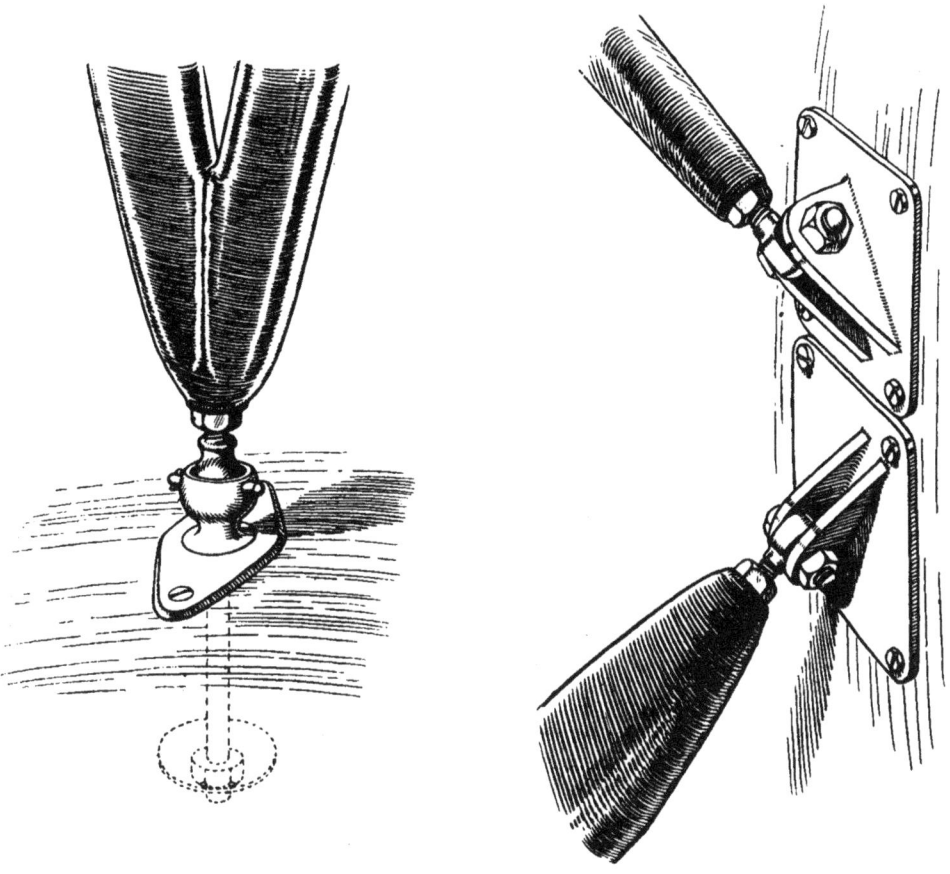

FIG. 3.   FIG. 4.

Figure 4 gives the outside appearance of the attachment of the steel struts to the fuselage side. It will be noticed that the ball-headed bolt is replaced by an ordinary eye bolt, which is attached to a forked lug by the use of a nut and bolt. A similar attachment, illustrated in Fig. 5, is used where the plane attachment for the "N" strut attaching fuselage to lower plane, is found.

FIG. 5.

Where this attachment occurs on the body the fuselage is strengthened by internal bulkheads. The Pfalz system differs from the Fokker D.VII. scheme, inasmuch as all struts are demountable. In the case of the Fokker it will be remembered that a pyramid of steel tubes is welded integrally to the fuselage frame.

AILERONS.

The design and arrangement of ailerons on the D.XII. model have evidently been found satisfactory, as there is no change in the present machine. So far as could be gathered without uncovering the aileron, the internal construction is also exactly similar. The alteration in the number of interplane struts has made it convenient to place the aileron king-post very near to the aileron's inner end. This is made clear in the photographs, from which it will also be seen that the usual German type of aileron lever has given place to a new type which is very similar to English practice. A sketch of this feature is given in Figure 6, which is self-explanatory. The fitting is made of welded sheet steel.

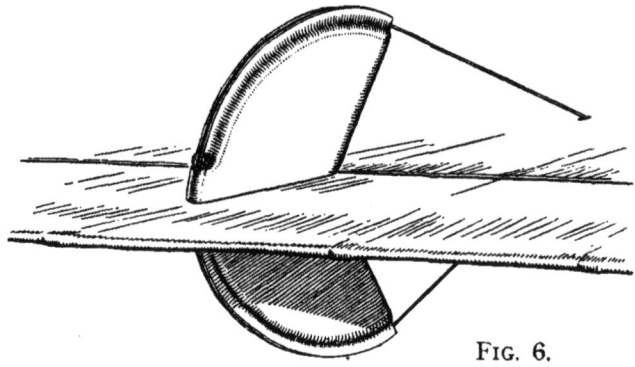

FIG. 6.

FUSELAGE.

It will be noticed that the D.XII. type of fuselage is in the main retained. This body was rather different from that of the earlier Pfalz D.III., and has evidently been found satisfactory in practice. The only alterations that affect the appearance of the fuselage is that the built-in type of fin, originally found in the D.III. but discarded in the D.XII., has again been incorporated; and that the tail skid is brought into line with modern German practice, as exemplified in the L.V.G.

The final version of the Pfalz body, which has always been of good stream-line form, is an excellent structure from both the aerodynamic and constructional standpoints. The actual construction has already been dealt with in the earlier Pfalz reports. The pilot's cockpit is very roomy and comfortable, and all instruments and controls are conveniently placed. A padded hammock seat is provided, which is sufficiently large to obviate the necessity for an adjustable rudder-bar.

UNDER-CARRIAGE.

This is the usual structure of steel tubing and is reminiscent in its placing of the Fokker under-carriage, but there is no auxiliary plane fitted to surround the axle. A section through the axle and fairings is given in Figure 7. The axle itself is a steel tube of 55 millimetres outside diameter. A

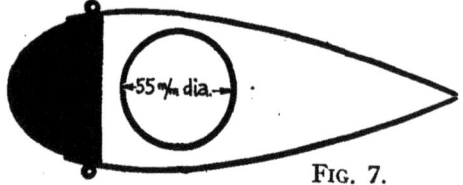

FIG. 7.

wooden strut of "D" section is fitted in front of the axle, and has its extremities housed in steel sockets attached to the under-carriage "V" by welding. The fairing is of sheet aluminium, and the upper portion is hinged so that it may rise with the axle on landing and taking off. The under-carriage bracing is the only external wire bracing to be found on the machine. The disc wheels are 760 mm. × 100 mm., and have the usual axle caps.

The upper extremities of the front under-carriage struts are attached one to each end of a steel strap passing under the fuselage, as is shown in Fig. 8.

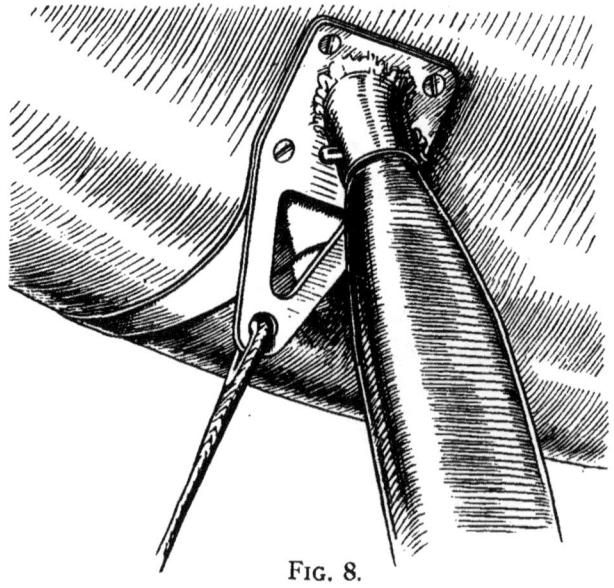

FIG. 8.

The aluminium doors illustrated in Fig. 9 allow either the lower plane or under-carriage to be dismantled without interfering with each other.

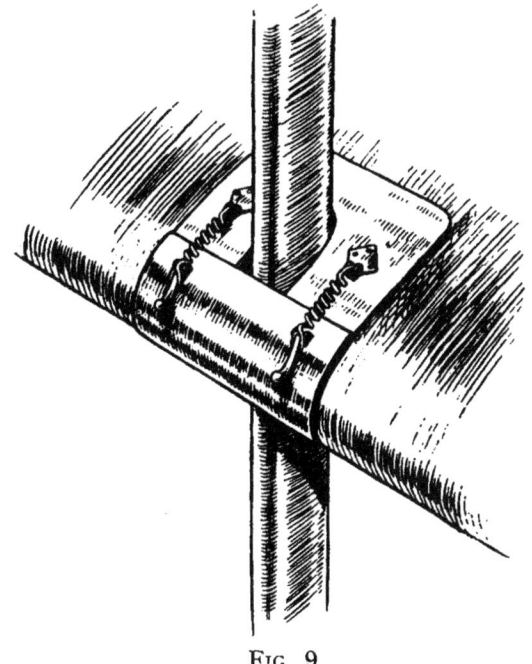

FIG. 9.

CONTROLS.

Figure 10 shows that the controls are very similar to those of the earlier Pfalz machines, but it will be noticed that the substantial sheet steel rocking lever which operated the aileron wires in the D.XII.

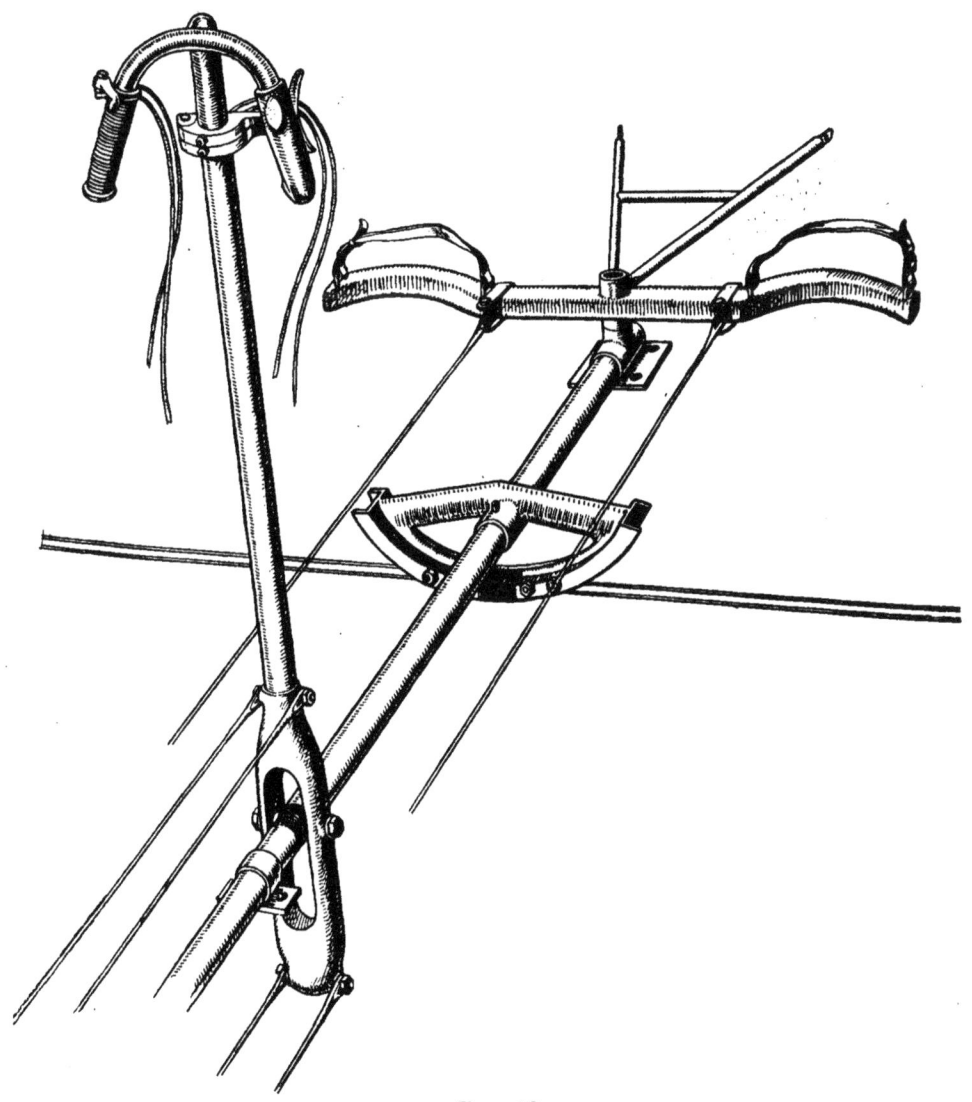

FIG. 10.

model is replaced by a much lighter fitting. The left-hand grip is a throttle working in conjunction with the quadrant throttle levers, while the right-hand grip is designed so that the gun triggers may easily be operated. The rudder bar is no longer provided with means of adjustment, and is very simple in design. As is common in German aeroplanes, it is built of sheet steel welded up. The aileron wires may be seen in Figure 1, passing through a hole in the fuselage top, just in front of the pilot, to the upper wing: turning on pulleys, the wires pass through the upper wing to re-appear just behind the rear limb of the interplane struts.

The upper elevator control wire passes through the fixed tail plane, otherwise there is nothing unusual about the elevator control.

The rudder control is as usual, but it will be noticed that the wires and levers are duplicated in the present model.

TAIL.

The shape of the tail plane and elevator has again been altered from the design employed on the D.XII. type. The scale drawing shows quite clearly the present shape, which, it will be noticed, is very similar to that of the corresponding member of the Halberstadt and L.V.G. machines. The fixed tail planes are of the usual three-ply construction, while the undivided elevator is a fabric-covered structure of light welded steel tubing. The rudder is of similar construction, and the arrangement of the steel tubing can be traced in the side view photograph. It is noteworthy that the German type of section, where the lower surface is of deeper camber than the upper, is adhered to.

The tail skid is of ash, with a steel shoe, and is of the entirely exposed type. The shock-absorbing material is the familiar triple-coil steel spring.

ENGINE AND MOUNTING.

The D.XV. Pfalz is fitted with a 200-H.P. Bayern motor. The engine bearers and mounting generally are exactly similar to that of the D.XII. There is nothing unusual to remark regarding the petrol and oil systems.

RADIATOR.

The D.XII. type radiator is retained, and it is worthy of notice that the aluminium blinker mentioned in the report on the earlier machine is still fitted. The radiator shutters—there are two halves—are operated from the pilot's cockpit, as in the earlier model.

ARMAMENT.

Two fixed machine guns are fitted, and are operated by the triggers on the control lever. Both are arranged to fire forward through the propeller path, and their mountings are of the usual Pfalz type.

COLOURING.

In the particular machine examined the body was painted a bluish-grey tint. The colour was not varied throughout the body, and no attempt at camouflage by means of stippling or broken colour had been made. The aluminium cowls surrounding the engines were left a natural colour. The fabric was of the usual printed-pattern type, except in the case of the rudder, where the fabric was left unpainted, and had simply been doped.

PROPELLER.

This is of the usual construction, and is of Axial make. It is marked as having a diameter of 2,650 mm. and a pitch of 2,400 mm., and carries the inscription " 200P.S. B.M.W. T.P., 1862A." The propeller

Fig. 11.

boss (*see* Fig. 11) is of the new type, already illustrated and described in I.C. 665—Report by the Technical Commission on German Aeroplanes and Engines.

February, 1920. G.T.C. (T.P.)

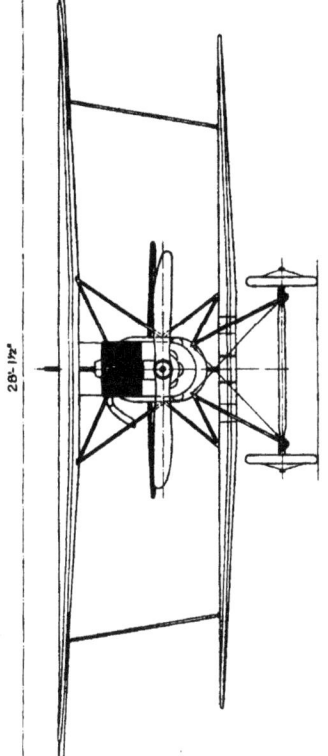
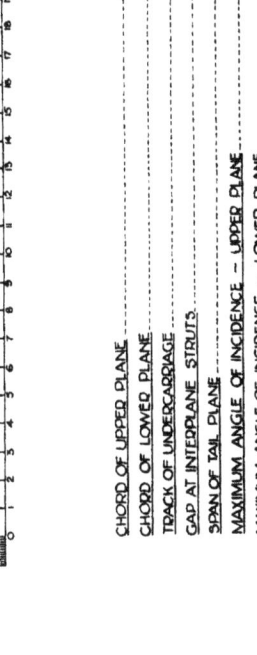

PFALZ BIPLANE
TYPE D.XV. 200 H.P. BAYERN

SCALE OF FEET

CHORD OF UPPER PLANE	4'-9½"
CHORD OF LOWER PLANE	5'-11½"
TRACK OF UNDERCARRIAGE	6'-3½"
GAP AT INTERPLANE STRUTS	5'-5"
SPAN OF TAIL PLANE	9'-2"
MAXIMUM ANGLE OF INCIDENCE — UPPER PLANE	2°
MAXIMUM ANGLE OF INCIDENCE — LOWER PLANE	3°

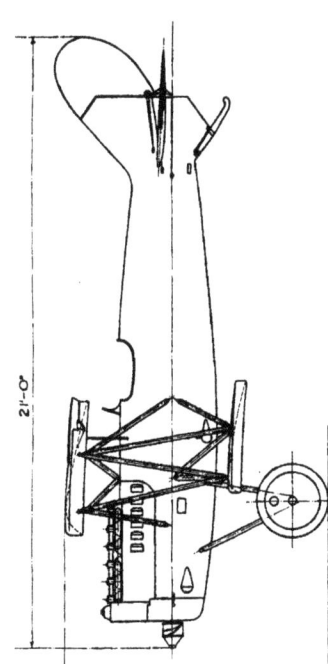
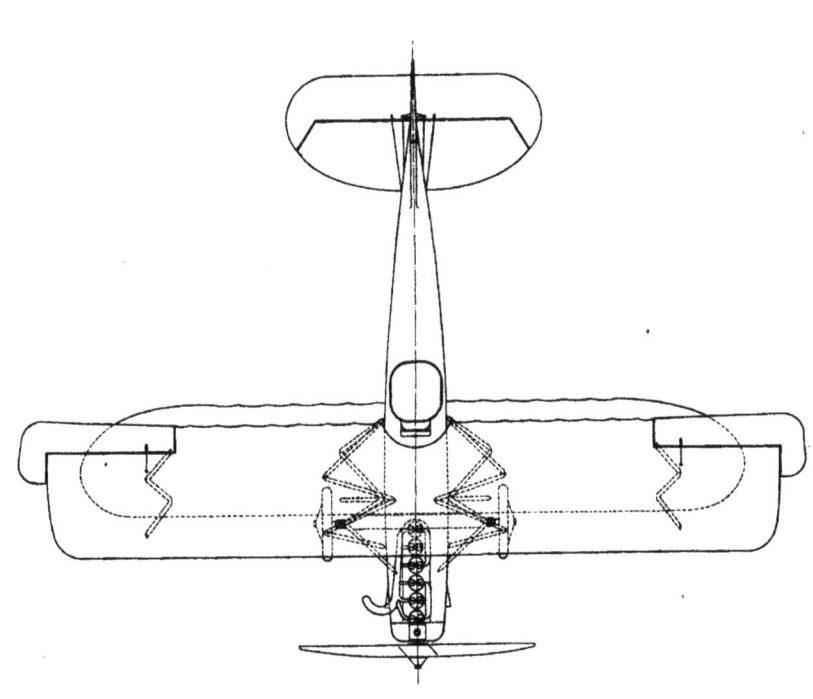

www.ingramcontent.com/pod-product-compliance
Ingram Content Group UK Ltd.
Pitfield, Milton Keynes, MK11 3LW, UK
UKHW051526180426
11947UKWH00019B/1593